THE BAR

A Discipleship Journal

Marcia Lebhar

Shrila,
With love and prayers.
Becky
Christmas 2014

Bare Branch Publishing

Jacksonville, Florida

Copyright © 2014 Marcia Lebhar

THE BARE BRANCH: A Discipleship Journal

All rights reserved. No part of this publication may be reproduced,
stored in a retrieval system, or transmitted in any form by means
electronic, mechanical, photocopying, recording, or otherwise,
without written permission of the author.

Publisher's Cataloging-In-Publication Data

Lebhar, Marcia.
  The bare branch : a discipleship journal / Marcia Lebhar.

  pages ; cm

  Summary: A collection of essays for the Anglican Gulf
    Atlantic Diocese.
  ISBN: 978-0-9913010-2-7 (softcover)
  ISBN: 978-0-9913010-1-0 (ebook)
  Library of Congress Control Number: 2014932801

  1. Christian life--Anglican authors. 2. Life--Religious
aspects--Christianity. 3. Attitude (Psychology)--Religious
aspects--Christianity. I. Title.

BV4501.3 L43 2014
248.4/83   2014932801

Cover Design by Shaun Lafferty

Bare Branch Publishing
3031 Secret Woods Trail West
Jacksonville, FL 32216

Printed in the United States of America
First Edition 2014

Contents

Introduction

My experience of knowing God is one of repeatedly, suddenly, *seeing*. Through the lens of his word in the Scriptures or through the compassionate intervention of the Holy Spirit, some conundrum is resolved, some burden relieved or disaster averted. There are, of course, the "crash and burn" examples when seeing seems to come too late. But seeing is always better than blindness. And we are often blind without knowing it.

Jesus promised recovery of sight to the blind. Sometimes spiritual insight comes as an answer to the sort of crying out the Scriptures urge the saints to do. Just as often, sudden sight seems to come unbidden, giving fresh perspective to the facts on the ground.

What follows is a collection of essays written for the Anglican Diocese of the Gulf Atlantic. As it happens, most of them are about looking at life through the Lord's lens.

~

All Bible quotations are from the New Living Translation, unless otherwise stated.

Supernatural Specs

Can those of you who are nearsighted, like me, recall the first time you ever put on a pair of prescription eyeglasses? I will never forget the shock of discovery, at age six, that the rest of the world could *actually see* individual leaves on a tree across the street from where they were standing. Other people had been seeing like this *all along?*

Perhaps because of this memory, I have always been intrigued by the drama of the servant of the prophet Elisha getting a pair of supernatural spectacles. 2 Kings 6 has the story of Elisha's servant awakening in the morning, emerging from his tent and discovering to his horror that he and his master are surrounded by enemy troops, horses and chariots. He loses it. He cries out to his master in despair. Elisha meets his servant's fear with faith: *"Don't be afraid!" Elisha told him. "For there are more on our side than on theirs!" Then Elisha prayed, "O Lord, open his eyes and let him see!" The Lord opened the man's eyes, and when he looked up, he saw that the hillside around Elisha was filled with horses and chariots of fire.* (2 Kings 6:16–17 NLT)

This panic-stricken young man was seeing an actual enemy army, not a product of a tortured or paranoid imagination. However, in a moment, his field of vision was eclipsed by a greater sight ... the armies of the Lord, poised to defend his own people.

Does anyone else identify with this servant, both in his panic and in what must have been his huge relief? I can think of countless times when some great fear of mine has been eclipsed by a gracious glimpse of God's even greater power at the ready to defend me. I need to remember to pray for this sort of vision when I am overwhelmed. I behave completely differently when I have my eyes trained on God's greatness rather than my fearful circumstances.

What about when others suffer? Notice that Elisha doesn't *explain* to his servant what he sees. Rather, he simply *prays* for his servant to see for himself what God is actually up to. Recently, more than one of our dear friends have experienced inexpressible trauma. We have learned, sometimes by our failure, the truth of Proverbs 25:20: *"Singing cheerful songs to a person with a heavy heart* is like taking someone's coat in cold weather or pouring vinegar in a wound." It is not always helpful to try to convey what we see. Instead, we can do as Elisha did ... pray for someone to see for themselves that God is at work. **Ask God to give them supernatural vision**. In the deep mystery of prayer ... he can and does.

This idea of *seeing supernaturally* is picked up in the New Testament. Paul promises that compared to eternity, our present sorrows are small and swiftly dissipating. In one impossibly ironic phrase from 2 Corinthians 4, he says we are to *"fix our gaze on things that cannot be seen."* At first glance this always makes me laugh. *Yeah, right*. Can we actually do this? Yes.

What does it mean to see cancer supernaturally? Or a child's illness ... or bankruptcy ... or infertility ... or violence and abuse of all sorts? It must mean that, like Elisha and his servant, we *see* that God *can* dramatically alter our circumstances. Their vision of the armies of the Lord wasn't merely encouragement about eternity. It was followed by an on-the-ground miraculous military reversal. We have to pray honestly for what our hearts desire.

Two years ago our pregnant daughter was told that the daughter she was soon to deliver would need cardiac surgery within hours of birth. The life-threatening condition was repeatedly confirmed, the C-section scheduled and arrangements made for a surgeon to be flown in from another city. But instead, from the moment of her birth, baby Miriam's heart began to heal spontaneously. She left the hospital on a normal schedule, with a healed heart. We *saw* God act in power.

However, here's a different kind of seeing: Just before the birth, our daughter said, "Of course we are praying for healing, but we are trying to trust the Lord with whatever comes. If there is a Kingdom purpose in this ordeal, then we want to trust God to walk through it with us and we want him to be honored." I will never forget hearing her speak those words. It's *just* what Paul was after when he said, *"For our present troubles are small and won't last very long. Yet they produce for us a glory that vastly outweighs them and will last forever! So we don't look at the troubles we can see now; rather, we fix our gaze on things that cannot be seen ..."* (2 Corinthians 5:17–18a)

The long list of saints and heroes of the faith in Hebrews 11 is a must-read. It plays with this idea of supernatural eyesight. Abraham obeyed God, leaving his home and living in tents for the rest of his life because he could see God's eternal home for him (v.10). Moses had the courage to walk out of Egypt, with the pharaoh pursuing in anger, because *"he kept his eyes on the one who is invisible"* (v.27). The chapter's victorious list then turns upside down and includes those who stayed faithful *in spite of* torture, imprisonment and murder. The author goes on to beg us to persevere in this life of faith, regardless of our circumstances, as if we were running a race. And what is to fuel our endurance? *"Fixing our eyes on Jesus ..."* (Hebrews 12:2). And when we fix our eyes on Jesus, what do we see? *"...Because of the joy awaiting him, he endured the cross, despising its shame."* (12:2)

Think of Jesus enduring Good Friday because he could see beyond it.

The Truth Is in the Trees

On the first day of classes, the students file in, sullen and guarded. They regard me with suspicion. I am daunted. Teaching required Bible and religion courses to students in a private high school has got to rank as one of the most intimidating—and most rewarding—challenges to which Jesus has ever treated me. Combine all the normal adolescent resistance to adult authority with the spirit of the age about organized religion ("You have *got* to be kidding me! *Please* do not even try to force-feed me this unscientific Sunday school junk!" ... This is cleaning up the language a good bit.), and you might get close to the hostility level of the first week's classes.

One of my favorite ways to pierce the resistance was with Paul's simple claim in Romans 1. The claim is this: The things God made, which surround us in his creation, speak so clearly and specifically of his nature that we are in some way held responsible for discerning that nature, just by being alive. What we can simply observe in our world ... reveals Truth.

They know the truth about God because he has made it obvious to them. For ever since the world was created, people have seen the earth and sky. Through everything God made, they can clearly see his invisible qualities—his eternal power and divine nature. So they have no excuse for not knowing God. (Romans 1:19–20)

So we began our study of the Book, without the Book. I hauled in a bag of "nature" for us to consider. Pinecones, leaves, seedpods, water and rocks. Everyone had something on his or her desk. As well, they were invited to look out the window and fix on something, anything, *animal, vegetable or mineral,* that was part of what the Bible claims makes up the created world. And then we made a list. If this were our only clue to the nature of God, without his glorious self-disclosure in his Word and his Son, how much could we actually figure out about him?

The lists turned out to be long, complex and lovely. And then students began to consider what else they knew about the created world. What could be seen through a microscope or a telescope? What does the study of microbiology or the structure of DNA tell us? What does our knowledge of the ever-expanding universe say? How do we understand the mysterious beauty of fractal geometry? What could it possibly mean to us that, through a complex process occurring during pregnancy, the body secretes a chemical that loosens only the hip joints of the mother about to deliver? What do these things speak about eternal realities? The Scriptures claim that creation is demonstrating Truth to us all the time, if we have eyes to see it.

Jesus was urging his disciples to *see what matters*, when he said, *"Your eye is a lamp that provides light for your body. When your eye is good your whole body is filled with light"* (Matthew 6:22). Jewish literature experts tell me that "a good eye" is an idiom describing generosity. How appropriate. Understanding the world as God's gift engenders generosity. The way we see our world, our circumstances and ultimately, ourselves, steers us.

The image of a bare branch in winter is one of my most poignant takeaways from this season. Stripped, unlovely, past fruitfulness, its life looks irretrievably ended. Hopelessly over. Defeated by cold. Don't *we* have these seasons? We have learned, watching and waiting, that this barren, apparent death is not what it seems. Green is on the way.

When the Scriptures exhort me to fix my heart on the realities of heaven, on the hope of the resurrection, or God's ability to redeem apparent disaster ... and when it seems too sweet or fantastic a thing to actually be true ...

I remember the bare branch in winter. God has put the promise on display before my eyes and in my years of seeing. The truth is in the trees, as well as in the Book, and seeing it with a "good eye" gives me courage to trust all my seasons to the Creator.

Bike Riding, Bible Reading

We spilled into our first sabbatical stop tired and out of shape in every way—physically, emotionally and spiritually. "There are bikes in the shed," our hosts told us. "Help yourselves." Hmmm. Maybe. One day, we ventured out deciding to ride to another town, carelessly not calculating the distance. I remember how grueling it was ... on how many hills I had to dismount and push the terrible thing ... how painful it was just to walk the next day. Still, we were mighty pleased with ourselves. Twenty-seven miles!

When we'd recovered from the initial shock and could move again, we chose another destination, more carefully this time. And another. And then another. Thus began a mutual love of bicycling. When we returned there a year later and again rolled the bikes from the shed to try our initial route, we shrieked with joy the whole way. Was this ever hard? How could we have thought so?

I remembered this at seven o'clock this morning when I began a run after a long hiatus, and two days before I wanted my jeans to be loose. My jeans won't be loose by this weekend, but if I don't give up today there's hope for next weekend. Layering ride upon ride, run upon run, there *will* be progress. The thing is to start, and then to start again.

When our son began to write music, this truth took a different shape. You can't write your tenth song first. It only comes after the first nine, which won't be as good. Don't be discouraged. Keep writing.

I always want the first coat of paint to be the last, though you almost always have to have a second coat before anything looks decent.

Now I see that this has been true of studying the Scriptures my whole life long. It is a layering process like everything else. Passage by passage, thought by thought. The more I look, the more I see. And the more I see the microscopic, the DNA, the more I see the whole, the macro, come into focus.

Joseph, the son of Israel who was rejected by his brothers and sold into slavery in Egypt, there rescues the whole Gentile world from famine. One day, his brothers themselves, now starving, journey into that Gentile world looking for food. Recognizing them, Joseph is overcome and stages a reunion. Removing, we assume, his Egyptian "disguise" and pledging his love and forgiveness, Joseph promises them that God has brought great good from their treachery. I will never forget first hearing this echo in Paul's promise (Romans 11), that the Jewish leadership's rejection of Jesus in the first century meant life from the dead for Gentiles. Then Paul promises what we have already seen in the Joseph reunion tableau ... that the Jewish brothers of Jesus will one day come, hungry, to the one they had cast out. Jesus is longing for that reunion. The macro is in the micro. The universe is in the cell.

The Israelites in the desert found that hoarded manna rotted. They were permitted no bank accounts and no insurance policies. God is enough. He will be tomorrow who he was today. Later, through Jeremiah (Jeremiah 2:13), God chastises Israel for digging cisterns next to streams of living water, hedging their bets *just in case* God forgets to be God ... or neglects to be good. God is enough. Will he not be tomorrow who he has been today?

Jesus' story of the servant who buries his master's investment makes the same point. Of what is the last servant afraid? He is afraid that his master will *"reap where he has not sown"* (Matthew 25:24–25). In other words, he is afraid his master will fail to supply him for what he is required to do ... afraid his master will ask him to bring in a harvest without giving him seed to plant one ... afraid God asks things of us which are too hard, if not impossible. So, *just in case*, he buries the treasure rather than using it. It is a warning about our hearts, and a thread of truth through the whole of Scripture.

The Author of Life is a *communicating* God who has built his truth into all creation and breathed it into his Word. Passage by passage, thought by thought. The more we look, the more we see. His Word is like the stable in Narnia, found at the end of C. S. Lewis' book, *The Last Battle*. It is far bigger within than without. The more it is explored, the vaster and more thrilling it proves to be. Nobody will ever really *know* it. Still, the more we look, the more we'll see. Layer by layer, God will show us what we need to see in his Word and of himself.

We learned years ago at our church that many adults shy away from adult education classes or Bible studies because they feel biblically illiterate and fear exposure. I want to apply our bicycle lesson to our Bible reading. Simply dust it off and hop on. There's a universe of love and wisdom in the smallest part. Passage by passage, thought by thought. It takes no time at all to be filled with awe.

www.oneyearbibleonline.com

You can go to this website and print out a Bible reading schedule. Don't worry where you start. Just start! Don't worry if you get behind. Pick up where you left off! Some people like to read Old and New Testament selections together. Some like to read a book at a time. Choose whatever you like ... choose and begin.

Before you read each day, ask God to speak to you through his Word. As you are reading, ask him to show you the heart of the passage and how it applies to your life. Some days will feel more vibrant than others. No worries; persevere!

He will answer you!

Wait!

There's something about having to wait that challenges each of us, and the way we wait tends to be revealing. My husband, Neil, seems to wait patiently for elevators. Why not? We can't make them come any faster. Me? I tap my foot, turn in circles and punch the button again and again. I multitask in the kitchen. Why not? It is possible to do three things at once. Just *watching* Neil do kitchen chores slowly and sequentially drives me mad.

Our rector's wife recently asked a group of disciples how well they *waited*. The question was intriguing to me. Uh-oh. Does it matter? She was reflecting on Abraham and Sarah and how deeply difficult it must have been to have to wait so long for God to fulfill his promise of a son. They did not wait well, as we all know, and Ishmael was the result. There came a point when they had waited so much longer than they had ever expected to wait, that taking matters into their own hands seemed the only way forward (Genesis 16). And moving things along ... doing something ... forward motion ... seemed the unquestioned necessity.

Since I flunked the "waiting question" quite badly, the idea of *how we wait* has become a new lens for me as I look at the Scriptures. Where do people ... and why do people ... have to wait, and what tends to happen when they do? So far, I have one observation to offer. It seems that waiting is a crucible. It tests us. It's when God's people have to wait that they get in trouble. The alternative to waiting for God is idolatry.

Think about the golden calf scene in Exodus 32. Why did God's people turn to idol building after all they had seen God do to free them from Egypt? Because Moses had been up on that mountain so long! They weren't expecting him to stay up there for forty days. They panicked. They couldn't stand waiting for him another day.

Once in the Land of Promise, it was when the rains they needed were delayed that the people turned quickly to idolatry, building Asherah poles and sacrificing to other gods, just in case those gods might come through faster than the one true God who had delivered them there.

On the road to Emmaus, Jesus made the claim that all the Hebrew Scriptures spoke of him (Luke 24:27), so it is fair to ask what these stories teach us about being his disciples. What are you getting tired of waiting for? Where are you tempted to give up while waiting for God to come through?

Waiting accentuates our helplessness, and that is what God seems committed to revealing. Only when we know ourselves to be helpless do we fully experience his grace and glory. We have to wait for it.

The people of Israel couldn't part the Red Sea. They couldn't bring water from the rock in the wilderness. Joshua couldn't take Jericho without weapons. Gideon couldn't defeat thousands with only a few hundred men. They couldn't bring rain to the Land of Promise. The disciples of Jesus couldn't save themselves in a storm or feed five thousand people with one boy's lunch. They couldn't bring their beloved rabbi back from the dead. They experienced helplessness, and *then* God put his glory on display.

Let me suggest that, as people whose hearts are inclined to *wait badly*, God has given us a way to practice the sort of helplessness that is helpful.

Sabbath. It remains one of the Ten Commandments. Right up there with the ones we consider the biggies, such as not committing murder or adultery. Why do we give ourselves permission to ignore this one?

Sabbath is like an enforced helplessness. It is a rehearsal in the waiting which God continues to require of us. It is a practiced alternative to taking things into our own hands. On the front end, it hurts. Leaving my to-do lists alone. Trusting the universe will continue its forward motion without my intervention. Demonstrating that it is God who sustains me and not my own efforts. Sabbath is like the scary free fall of faith, in microcosm. And it is good for our hearts to practice. It gets easier.

There is no legalism here. No one way to observe it. Sabbath still matters and we need the challenge it offers against impatience and idolatry. We need the practiced dependence it requires. And we need rest! We need God! And most of the time we are moving too fast to answer his call to be with him. This is the silver lining of the Sabbath cloud ... the profound security of his presence ... stopping long enough to remember how much he loves us. These help us *to wait* in larger ways.

~

I highly recommend Mark Buchanan's book on the Sabbath, titled *The Rest of God.*

White Hot Faith

One leader prayed such a radical prayer at a recent clergy gathering. Referring to Shadrach, Meshach and Abednego facing the furnace to which obedience in Babylon took them (Daniel 3), he prayed, "Lord, would you give us such *white-hot faith* that, without calculation and without hesitation, we would be bound and thrown into the furnace rather than displease you?"

My friends know that this Bible story is close to my heart. In my experience, there is always a "furnace" aspect to obedience, a fire to be faced, yet with joy waiting on the other side of the scary furnace door. Too often I am tempted to shrink from the door of obedience and, so, miss the celebration with Jesus on the other side.

We had some "vigorous fellowship" (euphemistic for heated discussion) when our family gathered one summer … conversation about what makes people willing to follow Jesus "without calculation and without hesitation." I suppose some calculation is appropriate in the sense that Jesus told us to "count the cost" of following him before we commit to it (Luke 14:28–30). Nevertheless, we agree with the sentiment in that leader's prayer, that we are hungry to see … *to be* … a Church that is passionate and radical, ready to follow wherever Jesus leads, whatever the cost.

So how do we get there? Increasingly, the Church in the West mirrors the surrounding culture. Statistically, our lifestyles, conversations, habits, spending patterns, even our divorce rates, are not distinctly different. Why isn't knowing Jesus making us braver … clearer… more radically loving?

One answer seems to be that we haven't really *believed* what we claim to believe. We haven't deeply understood the shattering, heartbreaking love of God for each of us. We don't take it personally—that the love expressed on the cross was just that—deep, personal, individual, forgiving love for *us*. It is a love that removes our guilt forever. *Ours. Forever. Gone.*

We don't take the power of the empty tomb personally either. What if we were willing to take *that* personally—to lean on the promise of the power that raised Jesus from the dead—as we go about our days? How would our lives change ... how would the world change ... if we cried out for a deeper experience of his love and power?

When Israel was similarly chameleon-like, reflecting the idolatrous cultures of surrounding nations instead of reflecting their God, Isaiah promised that God was just waiting *"to show you his love and compassion"* (Isaiah 30:18a). *"He will be gracious if you ask for help. He will surely respond to the sound of your cries"* (30:19b). It reads like a plea from God to call on him.

What if we each cried out to God for a deeper understanding of his love and compassion?

Now, here's the other side of our family's *vigorous fellowship*: (good Jewish thought is content to hold things in tension rather than to aim for synthesis or pure resolution.) *Often we come to an understanding of God's love ... to a greater vision of who he is ... by simply obeying him.*

Shadrach, Meshach and Abednego met the Lord, gloriously and profoundly, on the other side of the door obedience took them to. (Daniel 3:25)

Gideon had to be willing to drag his meager strength out of hiding and take some risks before he saw the God of Israel act in power for his people. (Judges 6:14)

When Jesus sent out his disciples on a ministry tour, they left in straightforward obedience, but came home elated! (Luke 10:17, 21)

For these saints, their vision of God's love and glory *followed* their obedience.

In John 4:34, Jesus says, *"My food is to do the will of him who sent me ..."* If the Church in the West is often listless, conflicted and bewildered, could it be that we are starving for lack of the *food* of obedience? Through neglect of "taking up our cross" in practical ways, have we starved ourselves of God's intended nourishment?

What if we each committed to asking, and then simply doing whatever God told us to do?

Where will we find that "white-hot faith" of which our leader spoke? Will it be in crying out for a deeper understanding of the love and power of Jesus? Or will it be in first obeying whatever he says to us and then discovering his love and power in response? Jesus' words to the Ephesians in Revelation 2 seem to say both! While he commends the Church for their stand for the truth and their patient endurance of suffering, he charges them with losing their first *love*. The antidote? *"Turn back to me and do the works you did at first"* (Revelation 2:4–5). It's not an either-or proposition. Renewing our understanding of the Lord's love and determining to obey him fearlessly are not in conflict.

I recently learned a quirky fact ... that when Europe was gripped with the plague in the fourteenth century, while multitudes were rushing out of the cities where disease was spreading, some Christians were streaming *in* to care for the sick in the name of Jesus. I want that same "white-hot faith" with which to meet the cost of discipleship in my day, a faith that has deeply understood the love of Jesus and is willing to be put at his disposal without reserve. They go together! May we *"spur each other on to love and good deeds"*! (Hebrews 10:24)

Do ... *Then* See

One of the most oft-repeated principles taught at a recent Anglican Church in North America conference was Bishop Todd Hunter's reminder: *Obedience precedes understanding.* The phrase is variously attributed to the Church Fathers, to George McDonald and to a host of others. And I thought I discovered it!

In the years when a large group of young adults met weekly at our house, the question of guidance was frequently at the forefront of their preferred topics for study and discussion. How do we hear God? Are you ever absolutely sure what you think you have heard is actually *from God*? How can people speak so easily about what God *said* to them? What if what I *think* I heard doesn't make sense to me?

As I searched the Scriptures for understanding, what I found there validated my own experience with stunning consistency. Notice how many biblical saints were given instructions which mystified them ... or worse, instructions which must have tempted them to think they had heard incorrectly, or that God was not actually *good*. Noah could not possibly have envisioned the need for the ark he was told to build (Genesis 6:9–22). How could Abraham not wonder whether he'd heard correctly when told to sacrifice his son (Genesis 22:1–2)? Moses must have doubted God's benevolence, or his own sanity, when he was asked to pick up a snake by the tail (Exodus 4:4). How about Joshua's bizarre instructions for the capture of Jericho (Joshua 6:1–5)? Jesus told his disciples to feed thousands of people with just a few loaves and fish (Mark 6:37). Or worse, he said that he must go to Jerusalem, not to finally overthrow the oppressive Romans, but to die. *What?* The disciples followed him, but they could not possibly have understood the deliverance God intended or the part they themselves would play in making it known (Luke 18:31–34). At least they couldn't see it on the front end.

And that would be the point for us as well. First we do ... and then we see. Do what you think you hear and then see what happens! Obedience precedes understanding.

My most fruitful adventures have followed this pattern. Once, while on a speaking assignment in South America, I received a very counterintuitive instruction from the Lord about sharing the Gospel with a person I'd just met. The nudge was heart stopping to me because it ran counter to the cultural norms of my host, and I imagined I'd dreamed it up. Even so, the Holy Spirit compelled me. The immediate result was a new sister in the Kingdom!

Back at home, I remember a particularly pedestrian example. I was driving home from the first of a series of Hebrew lessons at a local synagogue. As I was turning in to a fast-food drive-thru lane to pick up lunch, the Lord spoke to me. At least I thought it was the Lord: *I want you to fast for your Hebrew teacher.* Seriously? Maybe that was a perverse mental twist based on my hunger! I wrestled with the idea as I waited in the turning lane. Finally, dejected and full of uncertainty, I pulled out of the lane and drove home. All afternoon I alternated between faithful prayer and faithless (and hungry!) impatience. When could I eat again? Was that even God?

Before dinner, the phone rang. I will never forget it. My Hebrew teacher's heavy Israeli accent came through: "I have been going through the checks written for the class, and I see that your husband is a minister. Would you mind if I asked you a few questions about Jesus?" And my heart had been prepared.

Assuming that what we hear does not contradict the Scriptures, this is how we learn to hear the Lord, by doing what we *think* we hear and then seeing what happens.

It gets easier every time. When the prophet Malachi conveys the Lord's tithing challenge to his people, it reads like *obedience precedes understanding*:

"Bring all the tithes into the storehouse so there will be enough food in my Temple. If you do," says the Lord of Heaven's Armies, "I will open the windows of heaven for you. I will pour out a blessing so great you won't have enough room to take it in! Try it! Put me to the test!" (Malachi 3:10)

May we be distinguished by this kind of venturing obedience. Let's ask the Lord to teach us to hear him. Let's covenant together to do what we think we hear. Then, sharing our stories, we will fortify each other.

I declare your marvelous deeds. (Psalm 71:17 NIV)

~

For an interesting take on this principle, read the book by Clare De Graaf, *The 10-Second Rule.*

What's *Your* Empty Stable?

A little glimpse of Lebhar family history. Neil's fastidious mother and I were once working side by side in the kitchen of his childhood home. Neil was looking on. I was apparently being extra particular about whatever I was doing, because his mother suddenly teased me, saying, "Marcia, you are so neurotic!" Neil howled at the irony and immediately broke into the chorus of an old song titled, "I Want A Girl (Just Like The Girl That Married Dear Old Dad").

I do admit it. I'm a neatnik, a magazine straightener, a counter cleaner. I clean the house as we are leaving for a vacation so it will be fun to come home to. I love walking in and feeling *Aaahhhh!* Peaceful. Inviting. Clearly I am not apologetic about this. In fact, I have developed something of a personal theology to justify my housecleaning inclinations. Surely, order and beauty glorify God. Surely I am readier to open the door to friend or stranger if I feel like things are under control here.

Maybe. Opening the door invites all that order to come undone. Opening the door invites clutter and crumbs and complications. Bumps and breaks. Wear and tear. People and problems. The very ordering of my life under the roof of my house needs to be simultaneously offered back to God to be *disordered* or *reordered* by him. This is where God makes the conflicts of my heart clear. The *New Living Translation* renders the "double-minded man" of James 1:8 as one whose *"... loyalty is divided between God and the world."* All I am doing, I am doing for God, right? Still, does he have permission to mess up my house ... my life ... for a greater purpose?

Once when we were preparing for a wonderful wave of young adults to come in the door on a Sunday night, I felt particularly weary as I anticipated a long evening of serving and conversation and late-night cleanup. The Lord brought Proverbs 14:4 to my attention. It made me laugh *and* cry. *"An empty stable stays clean, but no income comes from an empty stable."* Half of my heart yearns only for an empty stable. No messy mooing and munching! Yet the better half of my heart wants Kingdom income to issue from the stable of my home and life.

Practicing hospitality is the obvious first application of this analogy and a challenge the Church in America desperately needs. Bringing the stranger, the outsider, into our homes and families is a profound way to demonstrate who God is and how he cares for us. Jesus cast much of his teaching in terms of shared meals and table fellowship. And his images for what he is doing now, as we await his return, are those of preparing a place in his home (John 14:1–4) and preparing a banquet for us, his bride (Isaiah 25:6–9 and Revelation 19:6–8). Though the book of Romans tells us to be eager to practice hospitality (Romans 12:13) and Paul makes enjoyment of guests in the home a qualification for leadership (1 Timothy 3:2), in this country we hardly ever do it. Neil is fond of quoting the statistic that over 50 percent of single Americans never enter another person's home in the course of a year. If we would be true disciples of Messiah Jesus, we'd open our doors.

Beyond the issue of hospitality, the image of the *empty stable* is a good shorthand way to help us talk about how else we might be arranging our lives according to divided loyalties. We want our email inboxes to stay under control. We want our schedules to stay predictable and sane, finances straightforward and unchallenging and career goals streamlined. What's your empty stable?

At the time of Jesus, disciples of an itinerant rabbi followed their teacher closely. They observed his every move. Being a good disciple was as much about imitating your rabbi's behavior as it was about learning doctrine. It involved mastering oneself as much as, or more than, mastering material. One of our favorite teachers says that learning how your rabbi responded to stubbing his toe in the dark was as instructive as memorizing his every word.

If you had slept in the same house or field with Jesus, awakened with him, eaten with him, walked with him and helped him, what would you have observed? One thing we always think of is that Jesus gave himself almost entirely to what *we* would consider interruptions. Most of the teaching, healing and wonders we see in his life were responsive ... seemingly unplanned. He trusted that what the Father allowed to cross his path was exactly that ... from the Father. Trusting his Father for the real plan for the day, Jesus always seemed willing for things to get messy.

Where's the profit, the Kingdom income, in the way we like our homes and schedules, in the way we arrange our lives? Sometimes it is only when we offer our *stables* up to be spoiled—from the world's perspective—that they really bring forth anything eternally valuable. Let's ask the Lord to give us grace to let him fill up our stables with whatever life-giving enterprises he knows we can handle. The Scriptures are clear that our stables are on loan and that one day we'll give an account of what has come from our use of them. It will not be enough to say we kept them neat.

Lists

I make lists. To-do lists. And then I feel so much better, even before I have actually done a thing. I make lists with paper and pen. Then I can see the progress of items crossed out. My husband makes lists in cyberspace. I think it must be far less satisfying to have the accomplished task simply disappear from the screen. It vanishes without a trace to remind him of the missions accomplished. My to-do list becomes a *have-done* list.

God makes lists. I love his lists. They are nothing like to-do lists. In Malachi 3:13–18, God's troubled people finally cry out to him with faith, directly, and they speak to each other about his goodness. He is listening and is so pleased, that he directs a "scroll of remembrance" be written to record their names for future celebration. Do you find that as astonishing as I do? Their prayers and their conversation about him have the power to encourage God! He makes a list!

The writers of Proverbs make lists. Proverbs 30 is a list of lists. Things that are never satisfied. Things that amaze. Things that make the earth tremble. Things that are small yet unusually wise. Things that "strut about"! The author is remembering and recording what he has observed.

Listing and remembering are related. Everywhere in the Scriptures we are urged to list and remember God's works, his mercies towards us. Of the Exodus experience, Moses says to God's people in Deuteronomy 4:9, *"But watch out! Be careful never to forget what you yourselves have seen. Do not let these memories escape from your minds as long as you live! And be sure to pass them on to your children and grandchildren."*

This is not a lame, nostalgic, blurry kind of remembering, however. Biblically, the word *remember* is muscular. Look at it this way: What happens when *God remembers*?

God *remembers* Abraham, and so saves Lot.
God *remembers* Rachel, and so opens her womb.
God *remembers* Hannah, and so gives her a son.

When Jesus promises to remember the thief on the cross, it isn't, "Oh, yeah! I remember that guy!" Rather, remembering him meant forgiving him and bringing him, faultless, to the Father.

So what does it mean for us to remember God's works? I believe it is similar. Remembering is an active, muscular endeavor for us. Remembering God's past acts of love and mercy fuels our lagging faith in the present moment, and it reverses despair. I love Nehemiah's call to the men of Israel, defending the newly restored walls of Jerusalem as the captives return: *"Remember the Lord and fight for your families!"* Remembering God's past wonders changes the present battle.

There's a powerful echo of this exhortation in Jesus' words to the seven churches in the book of Revelation. I made a list recently of *just* his instruction to each church, kind of peeled away from his description of each place, so that I could starkly see his charge to each church. The strongest common thread is an exhortation to *remember* and to return to what each church saw, heard and did *"at first,"* followed by the command to hold on to what they had left in order to prevent further loss and danger.

The whole scene assumes a progression over time *away from* Jesus and from ardent, active faith ... kind of a spiritual *Law of Entropy*. And Jesus' antidote is the same as the one we hear in Exodus and see played out in the wilderness accounts. It is essentially: *Remember who I have been to you ... what my deliverance has been ... what I have enabled you to do. Stir it up! Let those past demonstrations of my love and my faithfulness fuel your faithfulness now.*

To obey him, we will need to do some disciplined recalling. Like physical exercise, it strengthens us for what lies ahead.

A few years ago I faced a serious surgery. The part I dreaded most was the moment when I would be alone and helpless on a gurney, wheeled away from the protection and comfort of family. I confessed this to my kids, and they suggested I use those moments between parting and anesthesia to make a mental list of stories—stories of God's faithful intervention in my life. So I did it deliberately, and as I watched the hospital ceiling tiles roll by, I started cataloguing the Lord's gifts and wonders. My heart lightened. By the time we arrived at surgery, I was actually joyful and unafraid. Never will I forget this dramatic and swift change of heart.

What if, as individuals and as faith communities, we made this sort of *has-done* list of God's mercies? Would we see our trials differently? Would we share differently? Would we have greater courage as disciples? Psalm 145:11 says, *"They will speak of the glory of your kingdom; they will give [list?] examples of your power."*

This isn't a rosy denial of any present difficulties. It is a deliberate discipline to help prevent the dangers of which Jesus warns in Revelation. I hope we take it seriously.

Invisibility

We say he is the image of the invisible God (Colossians 1:15), yet even in his coming to us and taking on flesh, Jesus is still invisible. Willing to be invisible ... unrecognized ... unacknowledged.

You can hear the incredulity in the voice of his young friend, John, can't you? *"He came into the very world he created, but the world didn't recognize him"* (John 1:10). I try to imagine that pain. The breathtaking irony. The hunger to be known and understood. The longing for the world to *see*. The temptation to strip off his human prison of flesh and establish his identity, his worth, beyond all doubt.

For Jesus to become a creature in the world he created is more than enough to get our minds around. Lucy Shaw expresses the stunning wonder in her poem, "Mary's

Song": "Quiet he lies, whose vigor hurled a universe." But to make such a journey of rescuing love from heaven, to the utter helplessness of infancy ... and then be passed over ... misunderstood ... judged to be nothing?

What single-minded, purposeful, compassionate obedience did it take for Jesus to walk through this world completely unrecognized for who he truly was? Even those dearest and closest to him did not grasp it while he lived.

When he calmed the lake water of the Galilee, or changed the fresh water to fine wine, didn't he want to tell his earthly friends ... anyone ... what it was like on the second and third day of creation? What it was like to speak and have seas divide and waters spring up from the land?

And when he helped his friends to fish, did he remember the fifth day of creation, when fish first swarmed in the seas? Was it a burden to bear that nobody ... nobody ... *got it? Got him?*

The author of Hebrews says what kept him going was *"the joy set before him"* (Hebrews 12:2). The joy of accomplishing what had been lovingly planned from the beginning ... the joy of pleasing his Father. And you. Your face was before him. He was willing to bear the terrible irony of obscurity to accomplish the plan, to please his Father, and to win you.

Faces come to mind. Faces of friends who feel invisible and passed over. Faces of friends who are willing to serve Jesus in arenas which will never offer them anything like the recognition they deserve. Faces of saints who willingly, gladly, lay down the worldly accolade for the "Well done!" of heaven. Or who try to. Or who want to. How do they do it … the ones who do? How will we?

All of us, some frequently, feel undervalued and unseen. Yet, our deepest pains are lessened in that moment of recognition that Jesus … gets it. That his own feet have walked through this very pain. May we stretch to be like him, and live for his accolade alone, his face only before us. For soon, as Scripture promises, we will be face to face.

Eavesdropping

One summer my husband, Neil, and I had the decidedly unhappy task of admitting to ourselves that the shrubs to one side of our front door were dead and must be removed. A small team of people with hatchets and shovels made relatively quick work of the removal. Then we had a lovely, empty patch of dirt, all raked and ready to be replanted. The daily afternoon downpour interrupted us. When the rain ceased and we came out to resume the work, there in the dirt was a perfect illustration of my latest biblical rumination ....

The water had poured off the roof in sheets, creating in the un-mulched dirt a distinct, deep line under our front windows, as if someone had drawn it precisely with a stick. I wish I had taken a picture of it! That morning, I had been thinking of the places in the Scriptures where God seems to be *eavesdropping.* It is a crazy idea, I suppose, since he is omnipresent and even hears all our thoughts. Still, some Bible stories suggest the idea, so I looked up the word. The root, as you can guess, is that someone stands at your window, *as close as the line where water* **drops** *from the* **eaves** *of your house,* and therefore can hear all that you say inside.

Remember the wonderful scene of *mutual* eavesdropping in Genesis 18? The Lord, through three visitors, meets Abraham outside his tent and promises that Sarah, his wife, is soon to become pregnant. Abraham and Sarah were about a hundred years old at the time. Sarah is eavesdropping from inside the tent and has a good laugh at the thought. *"After I have grown old, and my husband is old, shall I have pleasure?"* (v.12, RSV) But God is eavesdropping on her eavesdropping! He challenges her for laughing. In what I have always heard as an affectionate conversation, Sarah denies laughing. God insists he heard her, and promises both Abraham and Sarah that he's *not* joking!

2 Kings 6 records another great eavesdropping scene. The king of Syria makes plan after plan to attack Israel. Each time, the Lord warns the prophet Elisha, and Elisha tips off the king of Israel. Furious, the king of Syria accuses his leadership of spying for the enemy. *"Which of you is the traitor?"* (v.11) Desperate, they reply, *"It's not us ... Elisha,*

the prophet in Israel, tells the king of Israel even the words you speak in the privacy of your bedroom!" (v.12)

Why do these scenes intrigue me? Several times over the years God has gently challenged me that even though I can be assured he hears my every thought, he nevertheless would like me to direct my cries *to him.* The Scriptures as well have taught me that we have the power to encourage the Lord, and even the saints and angels, as they eavesdrop on us!

Years ago I faced a stressful time in ministry work. I lacked the skills I needed. I lacked the people I needed. I lacked the money I needed. I began to awake in the middle of each night, coiled with anxiety. One night I gave up trying to sleep and went to the kitchen to make herbal tea. One of my daughters had brought a box of "Christian" tea home from college. Though I detest the idea of selling tea for twice its value because of a Bible verse on each teabag's cardboard dunker, I reached for it anyway. As I steeped my tea, I absent-mindedly glanced at my teabag. I was taken aback. Here is what it said: *"My people wail on their beds in the middle of the night, but they don't cry out to me from their hearts!"* (Hosea 7:14)

What? Was God speaking to me through a teabag? Clearly, he was. I would have told you that I was praying as I tossed and turned each night. It was not prayer, though ... only a vague awareness that God was eavesdropping ... that I was somehow struggling in his presence. He was challenging me to direct my angst specifically *to him*, even if it meant crying out. It is a subtle yet fundamental distinction. Chastened, I directed my cries to him, and within hours in the next day of work, my situation changed radically.

Confirming this lesson is a now favorite scene in the book of Malachi. The people of God are complaining to each other that their faithfulness to him seems to be doing them no good. The passage implies that God's people are suffering in some way, while his arrogant and faithless enemies "get rich." What's up with that? God is eavesdropping and he challenges them: *"'You have said terrible things about me,' says the Lord"* (Malachi 3:13). They deny what he has clearly heard, just like Sarah! The Lord persists, playing their conversation back to them. He provokes them to complain to his face. What is the point here? God can hear our grumbling to each other, even our inner wrestling. Even so, he wants us to direct those comments to him. Only then can we receive his answers and appreciate his purposes.

The best part is still ahead. Malachi continues: *"Then those who feared the Lord spoke with each other, and the Lord listened to what they said. In his presence, a scroll of remembrance was written to record the names of those who feared him and loved to think about him."* (v.16)

Imagine. Not only is God listening, but also our thoughts toward him and our conversations with each other about him have the power to encourage him. He makes a list! He promises to reward them!

There's more. The writer of Hebrews (12:1) tells us that we are surrounded by a huge crowd of saints who have gone before us. The saints of the Hebrew Scriptures longed to see our day, when the Messiah, Jesus, had accomplished the redemption they could only see from a distance. Like onlookers who have been part of a relay race, they cheer us on, encouraging us to keep our focus on Jesus, our savior and bridegroom, as we all await our final reunion with him. Peter tells us... *"that even the angels are eagerly watching these things happen"* (1 Peter 1:9). Along with the Lord, they watch and listen until we are all at the wedding banquet together.

God and the heavenly host with him are all listening to us! The heavenly pencil is sharpened and the list of those who treasure him and turn their faces toward him has begun. Let's turn our thoughts, and even our cries of complaint, to him, and make sure our names are on that precious list.

Naomi's Dream

The churches of Rome defy description. Beauty beyond compare. The architecture swings between cleanly simple and fabulously ornate. Most buildings alone are stunning, graceful, mind-boggling architectural feats. And within, sometimes even well hidden within, lie the most astonishing treasures. Caravaggio paintings unfold biblical scenes with breathtaking glory, subtlety and nuance. Bernini sculptures make marble move and breathe and speak.

Further, observant tourists are rewarded with the unveiling of another cast of characters. Visible from the naves, flying overhead or peering from around corners are chubby cherubs, whimsical lions and peaceful doves ... animals of all sorts and dispositions. Even skulls and skeletons lurk about, emerging from the walls to remind us that "all flesh is grass" and that our days on earth are numbered.

It is all so expressive and sublime, and yet ... *inanimate.* What is harder to find in most of Rome's churches, it turns out, are actual worshippers.

As our days in Rome drew to a close, I grew heavyhearted. All this glory, created to give God glory, and yet there was this echoing emptiness everywhere. Who was doing it? Giving God glory, that is.

Next stop, Nairobi. As we approached the cathedral for the opening service of GAFCON (Global Anglican Future Conference), the comparison was stark. Simple gray stone and exposed mortar. Unadorned. Walking beside me was my daughter-in-law, Naomi. She had grown up in a nondenominational setting in Japan, and this was her first experience of a cathedral. It would not be like the cathedrals of Rome.

As we entered in the narthex at the rear of the sanctuary, the scene broke over us like a wave. First was the sound of worship: drums, instruments, voices ... washing over us ... raising the roof. Then, a feast for the eyes. A human masterpiece. Added to the purple-and-red vestments of hundreds of bishops from around the globe, African women's bright dresses and headdresses bloomed like myriad tropical flowers throughout the nave. And this time the scene was ... *animate*! It seemed to move in unison as the strong wind of the Spirit blew among the worshippers.

Overwhelmed, we moved slowly down a side aisle, looking for a place to land. Suddenly Naomi clutched my arm and whispered, "I saw this—in a dream! It was years ago and I didn't know what it was! I saw the big table in the front and I thought the room was a courtroom. And I wondered why there would be so many people rejoicing in a courtroom. I never understood it, but I remember it clearly. It was *this!*"

It was a startling memory. But what did it mean?

Days later we gathered with friends to prepare a side chapel of the cathedral for a private confirmation service for Naomi. Being confirmed as an Anglican was a way for Naomi to say to her new husband, Peter, *"Thy people shall be my people ..."* (Ruth 1:16) and to confirm her calling to work alongside him. Naomi's dream was clearly in some way a confirmation of its own. Still, what did it mean?

Naomi joined us, radiant from some quiet moments with the Lord before our service began. "God explained the dream to me," she told me quietly. "It *is* a courtroom and God is the judge. We are guilty ... convicted. But when we go up to the rail and hold out our hands, because of what Jesus has done we receive a pardon—an acquittal instead of a guilty verdict!"

I may never again take communion without remembering that I am *"approaching the judge's bench"* and receiving my acquittal because of the love and agony of the one who suffered my sentence in my place.

"For the Lord is our judge, our lawgiver, and our king. He will care for us and save us." (Isaiah 33:22 NLT)

"For the Son of Man will come with his angels in the glory of his Father and will judge all people according to their deeds." (Matthew 16:27)

"There is no judgment against anyone who believes in him. But anyone who does not believe in him has already been judged for not believing in God's one and only Son." (John 3:18)

What Naomi saw in visual terms, J. I. Packer has described in theological terms in his classic, *Knowing God.* He says: *"Our judge has become our Savior .... Justification is the truly dramatic transition from the status of a condemned criminal awaiting a terrible sentence to that of an heir awaiting a fabulous inheritance."*

What Packer describes in theological terms, C. S. Lewis describes in narrative terms. The creatures of Narnia, turned to stone by the spells of the White Witch, live again as the breath of Aslan, the Lion, revives them. Breathed *upon*, they breathe, and return to flesh and blood and to jubilation at his victory over evil.

When God chooses unlikely young David to be Israel's king, he says, *"People judge by outward appearance, but the Lord looks at the heart."* (1 Samuel 16:6–8) Judging by outward appearance, there would seem to be no comparison between the cathedrals of Rome and Nairobi. But God, give us Nairobi hearts! Make us *living stones* (1 Peter 2:5), alive with the irrepressible elation of those who have been both credited with righteousness and loved back to life.

Know That I Know

A year of grieving losses was about to close for our family. Twice in one year we sat beside a dying loved one. The first was my husband's mother, and then my sister. Both times we wondered what each woman knew, or remembered, of spiritual realities.

Every death serves as a reminder of our own mortality. As we watched and waited, twice, I thought of the teasing request I had once made of my children. Among life's most poignant joys to me have been the rare occasions when they are together, making music. I once made them promise to *sing me out*, if they got the chance, when my time comes. The memory prompted the following reassurance:

Know That I Know

When it's my turn
Like the flowers by her bed
To fade
To shrink
To leave just the stark and shriveled stalk
All the rich wonder of the colors gone
Know that I know

Know that I know
That fear lies
And the truth is in the trees
Though the branch is stripped
By winter gripped
Still death is a deceit
Radiant green will yet burst forth
And sing praise to the loving hand
Of its maker
Know that I know

Know that I know
That through the mercy of another tree
My sins and sorrows will fall like leaves in winter
Gone forever
Then all that was promised
All that was best
Will bud and never fall
Will celebrate
And wait for you
Know that I know

Know that I know
But even so
Sing me your gentle reminder

About the Author

Marcia Lebhar is a storyteller and exhorter with a passion to see "ordinary" believers in Jesus encouraged, challenged and equipped to walk with God on his extraordinary paths.

The wife of the Anglican Gulf Atlantic Diocese's first bishop, Neil Lebhar, Marcia has been actively involved in lay ministry since her college years. Marcia attended George Washington University, Princeton University, and Albertus Magnus College, earning a B.A. in English with a secondary concentration in Religion.

Marcia came to faith through the secondary school ministry of FOCUS. As a FOCUS leader, an associate staff member for InterVarsity Christian Fellowship, a Bible teacher in both churches and secondary schools, a speaker nationally and internationally and as a discipler of the saints under her own roof, Marcia's passion has always been to share the treasure of the Scriptures. Her column, Discipleship Journal, can be found on the website of the Gulf Atlantic Diocese *(http://www.gulfatlanticdiocese.org/ discipleshipjournal).*

In 1981, the Lebhars traveled to Israel on a study tour associated with CMJ (Church's Ministry among Jewish people), based at Christ Church in Jerusalem. They have since led countless trips to Israel and both say that few things have had a more profound impact on their own lives as disciples, or a greater impact on their church. Marcia served as the American Director of CMJ during a period of rapid expansion. Apart from her role as parent to four and grandparent to six, her role as frequent Israel study tour leader may still be her favorite.

Profits from the sale of this book will support church planting in the Gulf Atlantic Diocese of the Anglican Church in North America.

CPSIA information can be obtained at www.ICGtesting.com
Printed in the USA
LVOW13s1045300614

392324LV00003B/3/P